RAMADAN

EXPLAINED TO CHILDREN

Author: Karima Kebir
Translator: Adam Bend
Edition: March 2024

Copyright and Non-Permission Notice

© 2024 -Karima Kebir

ISBN 978-2-925473-01-5

Edited by Karima Kebir, Ottawa, Ontario, Canada.
Published in March 2024.

Summary

Introduction

Ramadan is the ninth month of the Islamic calendar. Muslims worldwide observe this holy month as a time to deepen their connection with God and bring families together with hearts full of joy, and learn valuable things like patience, sharing and generosity.

Muslims perform an extraordinary feat during the month of Ramadan: they abstain from food for the entire day, from sunrise to sunset. They are prohibited from eating or drinking anything during this time, and they must also refrain from engaging in any negative behaviors like lying, cheating, or making fun of others.

Generalities

-2-

During Ramadan, it's a great chance to learn how to be kind, share with others, and pray a lot.

Muslims donate food to impoverished individuals, help those in need, and pray frequently to thank God for all that they have been blessed with.

This book is meant to help us understand what Ramadan is, what people do during this month, and why it's a unique and enjoyable time for children like you!

Are you ready for this exciting journey? Let's go !

The crescent moon of Ramadan

Did you know that the month of Ramadan starts with an extremely special event in the sky? It's the new moon!

Picture yourself gazing up at the sky at night and observing a narrow crescent of light shining brightly. This is the sign that Ramadan is about to start!

Every year, Muslims are filled with excitement as they look forward. It's like a little gift from the sky to say that it's time for families to prepare for a month of Ramadan filled with prayers, sharing and good deeds.

Sahur
"Pre-dawn meal"

Sahur is a meal that is particularly special and is eaten before sunrise in Ramadan.

During the early hours of each morning, when everyone is still asleep and the sky is dark, Muslims wake up to eat breakfast before the day's fast begins.

Sahur is crucial as it serves as a source of energy for people to make it through the day without eating or drinking while still feeling strong. It's akin to fuel for the body!

From now on, whenever you hear about it, you'll be able to understand what Sahur is!

Prayer during Ramadan

Muslims place great importance on prayer during Ramadan, as it is a chance to connect with Allah and strengthen their faith.

Did you know that Muslims pray five times daily? Yes, it's true ! They stop five times throughout the day to pray and communicate with Allah.

Among these five prayers, there is a very special prayer called Salat al-Fajr. This is the dawn prayer, which Muslims perform just before the sun rises. This prayer is very important because it helps Muslims start their day with faith and gratitude in their hearts.

Besides the mandatory five prayers, there are also optional prayers known as Salat Nawafil. Muslims attempt to pray as many Salat Nawafil as possible during Ramadan to earn even more blessings and rewards, while also displaying their love and devotion towards Allah during this holy month.

Charity during Ramadan

In Ramadan, Muslims practice charity by sharing what they have with those who need it. It's equivalent to showing some love and kindness to others.

There are many ways to give charity during Ramadan, including giving food to hungry people or offering something to a fasting person to break their fast, some individuals those who provide money or clothing to those in need, and there are others who give their time to help others. The key to giving is doing it with love and generosity, regardless of how you do it.

Muslims make an effort to give their best during this special month, believing that every act of charity is significant and blessed by God. Showing love to others and expressing gratitude to Allah during the month of Ramadan is what it is about.

Iftar
"Breaking the Fast"

When the sun goes down and everyone is extremely hungry, the awaited moment of Iftar arrives!

During Iftar, Muslim families gather together around a table to break their fast by eating and drinking. It's like a feast filled with delectable treats! The tables have a variety of delicious foods on them, such as sweet dates, hot soups, savory dishes, and refreshing drinks.

Iftar is a time to celebrate the blessings of Allah. Families pray together and express their gratitude to the good Lord for the food he has given them, as well as for all the good things.

Reciting the Quran during Ramadan

During the holy month, Muslims frequently read the Quran, a book that is very important to them. It is like a guidebook that provides wisdom and instructions that Muslims need in their lives. They are taught how to live a life filled with peace and happiness by being kind, compassionate, and generous to others.

They read verses from the Quran every day, and sometimes even all night. They attempt to comprehend what each verse means and how it can help them become better people.

The Quran's every word, or rather every letter, is a means of blessing and bringing Muslims closer to God. This is a way to celebrate this holy month and strengthen their faith in Allah.

Good deeds during Ramadan

Do you realize that in Ramadan, every good deed we perform is significant and counts more?

During this holy month, blessings are multiplied. This means that any good deeds, like helping someone, sharing, or being kind, are multiplied. Allah gives us even greater rewards during Ramadan! It's like our good deeds are magical!

Why is it so special? Well, that's because Ramadan is a month where we try to be the best versions of ourselves. We fast, we pray, and we do our best to be good, and kind to others. And Allah sees all of this and rewards us with even more blessings.

Laylat al-Qadr

Do you know that there is a very special night during Ramadan called Laylat al-Qadr or Night of Destiny? During this night, our Prophet Muhammad (peace be upon him) received the Quran, the holy book of Muslims, from the angel Gabriel (Jibrīl) in the cave of Hira.

Laylat al-Qadr is an odd-numbered night during the last ten nights of Ramadan, and it is very important because it is worth more than a thousand months!

Allah opens the doors of heaven and responds to the prayers of those who call on Him during this night.

Muslims dedicate this night to praying, reciting the Quran, and requesting Allah's blessings.

The benefits of fasting

The fast that Allah imposes during the holy month of Ramadan not only allows us to connect with God, but also provides many benefits to our body.

By fasting, our digestive system can be cleansed and our mind can be purified. Additionally, fasting provides our body with a chance to rest and regenerate. We are providing our body with a break it deserves to operate at its best.

Fasting also teaches us discipline and self-control, qualities that can be very valuable in our daily lives.

The act of fasting for several days in a row during Ramadan enables us to maintain our physical and mental health, which is crucial for leading a happy and balanced life.

Live actively during Ramadan

During Ramadan, it is essential for Muslims to stay active. They are encouraged to maintain a regular, active life instead of sleeping all day and waking up just before Iftar.

This means, among other things, working, shopping, playing sports and participating in physical activities such as cycling, football or swimming, without neglecting to stay engaged in social and family activities.

Staying active is key to keeping our bodies and minds healthy, strengthening our discipline and willpower, and appreciating the blessings of this holy month even more.

So, rather than spending the day sleeping, let's make the most of every moment of Ramadan and make it a memorable and enriching experience.

Patience and gratitude

During Ramadan, Muslims acquire two crucial skills: patience and gratitude. But what does this mean?

Patience is the ability to wait calmly and without complaint, even when things are challenging and difficult.

Being grateful is the act of saying 'thank you' for everything you possess and feeling content with what you receive.

Fasting can be difficult, since Muslims refrain from eating or drinking anything during the day, even if they are hungry or thirsty. They do not complain because they are aware that it is a test meant to strengthen their will and patience.

Muslims have a belief that God loves those who are patient and grateful, which is why they strive to be patient not only during Ramadan but also throughout their lives.

The end of Ramadan "Eid al-Fitr"

The Eid prayer is a special prayer performed in the mosque on the day of Eid al-Fitr. Muslims wear their best clothes and gather together with family and friends at the mosque to pray and express gratitude to Allah for the blessings they have received during Ramadan.

After the prayer, people greet each other by saying "Eid Mubarak!", which means "Blessed Eid!" or "Happy Eid!". Then, it's time to get together with family and friends to share a festive meal. The tables are filled with delicious traditional dishes, sweet cakes and delicious treats.

During Eid al-Fitr, children are frequently given gifts and money by their families as a reward for their diligent fasting and prayer during Ramadan.

Zakat "The charity of Eid al-Fitr"

During Eid al-Fitr, Muslims practice a special form of charity called Zakat al-Fitr.

It involves giving food or money to needy people just before the Eid prayer as per Allah's instructions.

Zakat al-Fitr is a way for Muslims to ensure that every person, regardless of their circumstances, can celebrate the holiday with joy and dignity, even if they are in need.

Muslims share their happiness and abundance with those who are less fortunate, which strengthens bonds of solidarity and empathy within the community. Ending the month of Ramadan with a beautiful act of showing gratitude to Allah and taking care of others is a wonderful way to do it.

Conclusion

Never forget that Ramadan is a time of sharing, love, and generosity. It's an opportunity to strengthen our family bonds and help those in need.

Whether it is fasting, praying, sharing or reciting the Quran, every act we do during Ramadan is a way of showing our love and devotion to Allah.

My wish for you is to keep learning and growing in your faith throughout your life. May Ramadan always bring you peace, joy, and happiness!

Ramadan Kareem!

With love,

Karima Kebir

COLORING
RAMADAN THEME

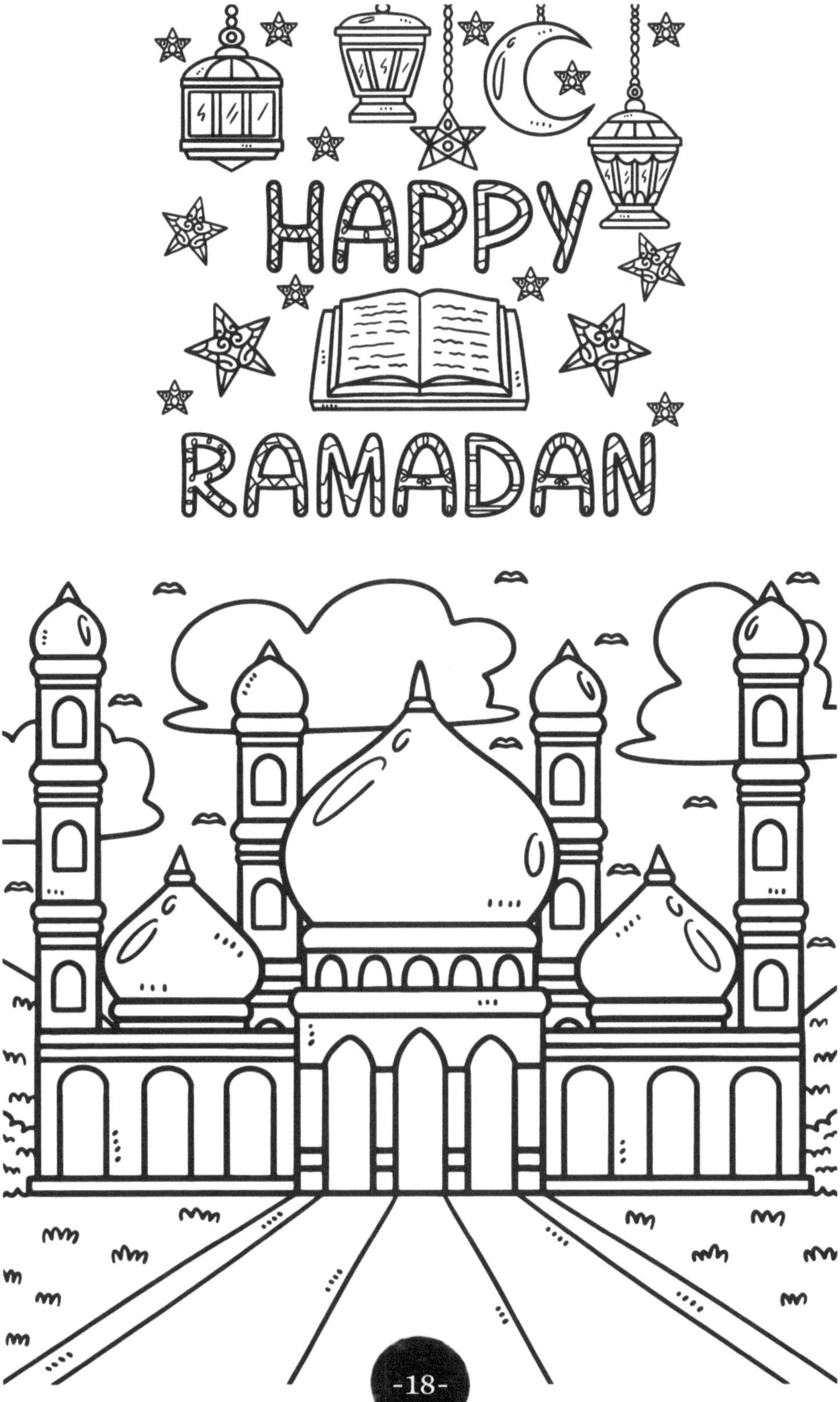

HAPPY
RAMADAN

رمضان مُبَارَك

RAMADAN KAREEM

HAPPY RAMADAN

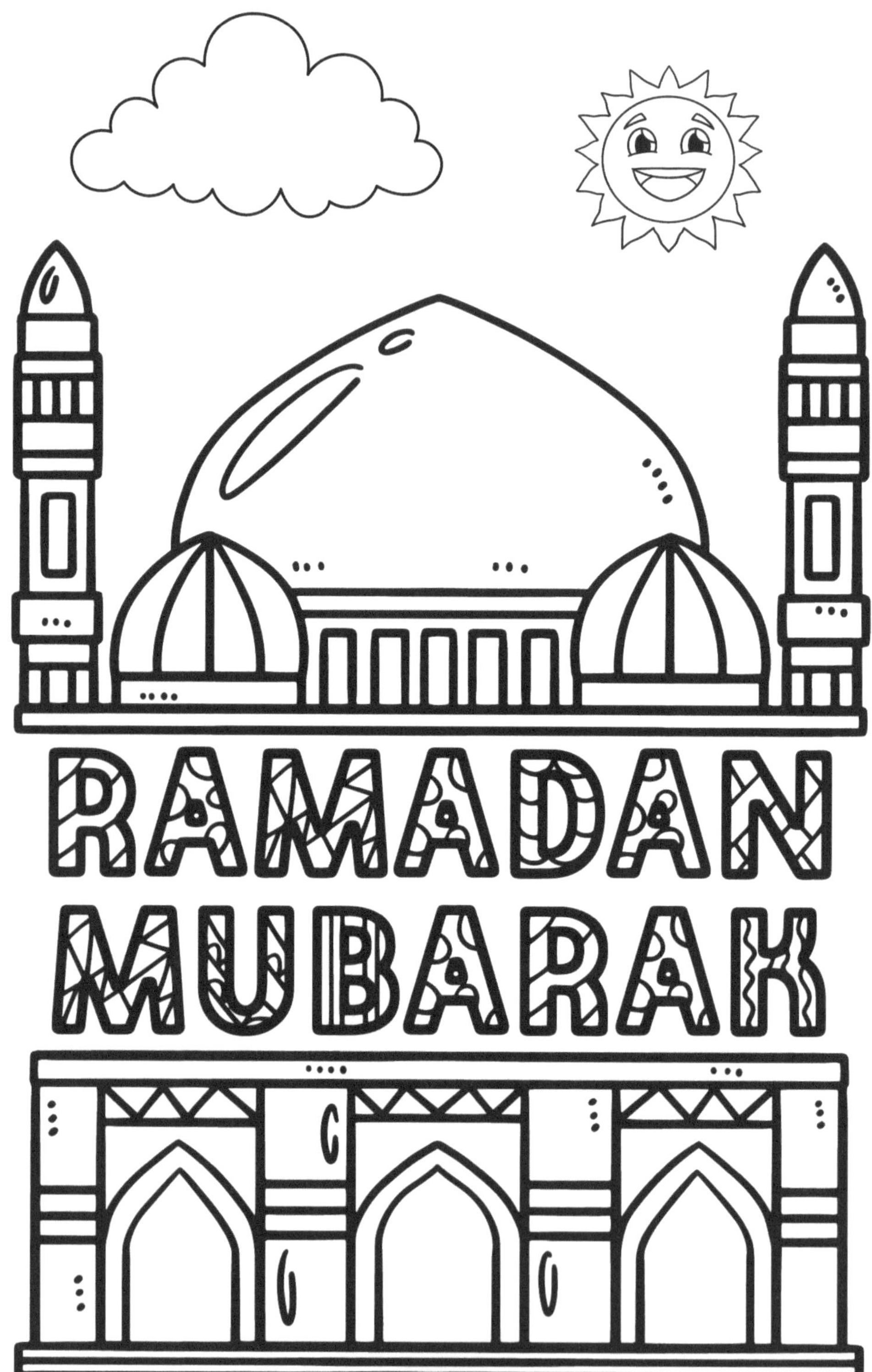

RAMADAN
MUBARAK

HAPPY
RAMADAN

Questions about Ramadan

1. What is Ramadan and why is it important to Muslims?

2. What do Muslims do during Ramadan?

3. What is the holiday that marks the end of Ramadan?

4. What does Laylat al-Qadr mean and why is it special?

5. What do you hope to accomplish during Ramadan after reading this book?